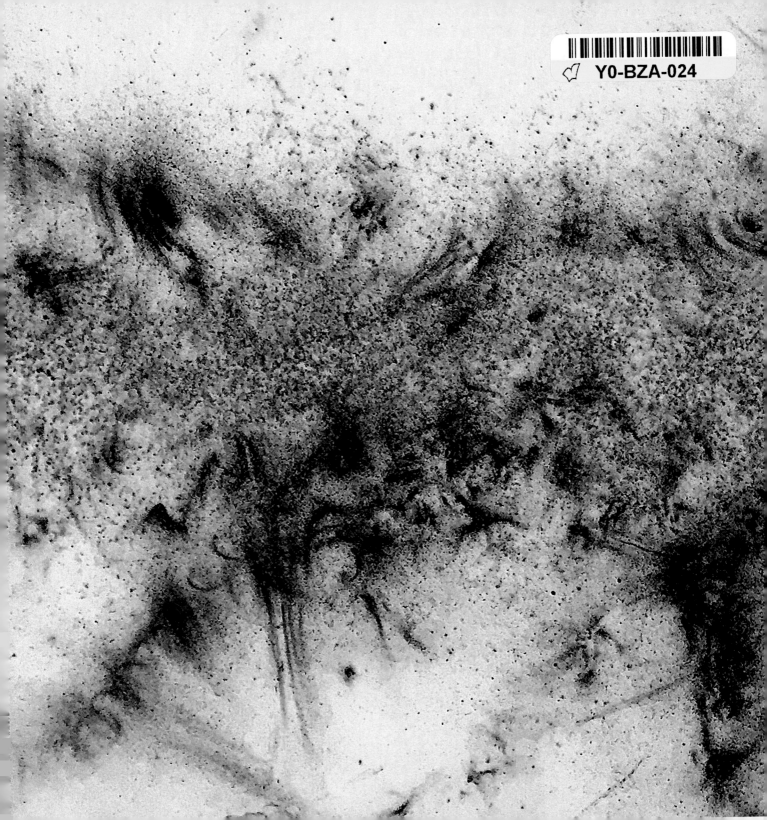

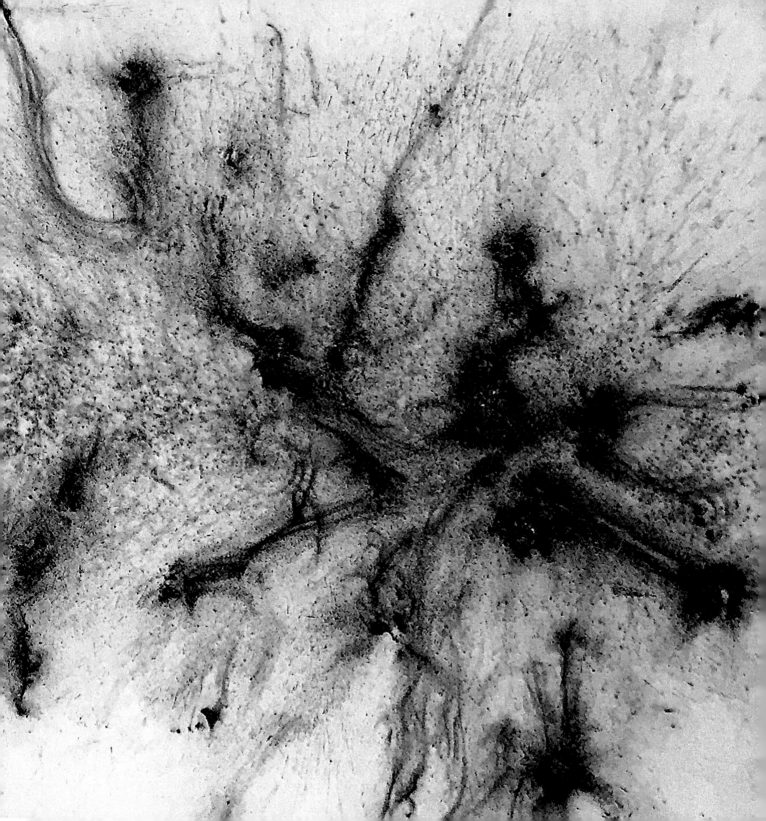

True Love and Smoke
by Christopher J.T. Kade Schmidt

Printed in the United States of America

First Printing, 2016

ISBN-13: 978-0692634523
ISBN-10: 0692634525

J.T.Kade
Portland, Maine

View me as a force to converse with.
View me as a spirit that loves, cherishes,
guides, and always will support you.

I said I begin to feel alright now.
I feel like I can tell you about my baby right now.
I said, I feel like you in the mood for me to tell you about my baby right now.

Sometimes, me and my baby
we fuss and fight,
and my baby leave home
cause things ain't right.

Oh but I get that feeling, so all alone,
and I call my baby on the telephone.
I finally get somebody on the telephone
and I say "Who is this,"
somebody say this is the operator.

I say "I don't want you operator. I want my baby!!
Oh operator...I want my baby!!"

And finally the operator get my baby on the telephone
and children, the minute I hear my baby say hello,
something start to move down inside me.

And now say I got a message for you honey
I wanna tell you that darling you,
      you send me.

      -Sam Cooke
     "Live at the Harlem Square Club, 1963"

Table of Contents

In the stillness of the mind I saw myself as I am - unbound.

-Sri Nisargadatta Maharaj

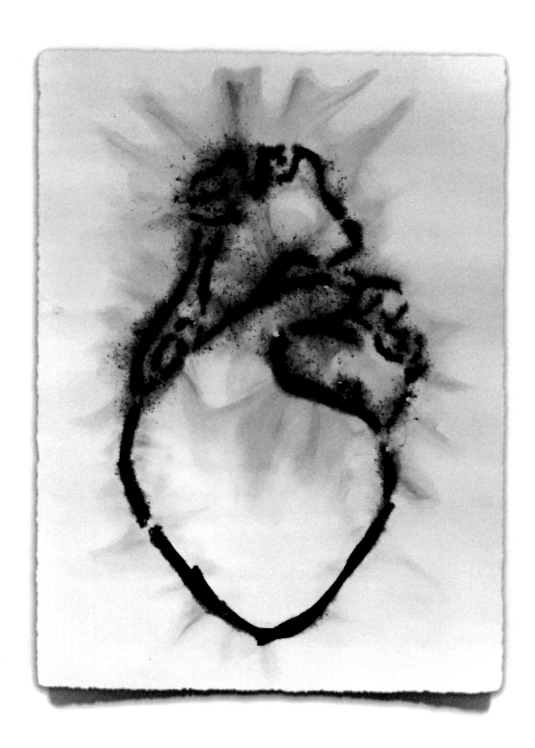

I don't know which weighs more on me, time or distance.
I've written stories of you, my inevitable girl next door,
but I realize our continents never touched.

My longing lies beneath the unoccupied nets of my eyes
in a vocal anguish that doesn't need language to give me permission.
But my latin derivation is you. The base of every word,

the sultry origin of thoughts, a memory of lips
wanting to tumble into each other across oceans, though
our time has not come to be   anything,   yet.

You, my weekend love always around the lighthouse   spinning,
your long legs setting all the tall ships of my blood sailing,
every moment just blue bread spread with sweet expectation.

Another sunset passing peels open my eyes with proof
that another day, quiet with your silence, means we will spend the night
apart, whispering candlelight colors to cool cotton sheets

hoping the slope of the neck, my new sky, would echo them back.
You, just a form, a photograph inside a phone that holds
millions of pixels and the labor of a million minds,

all so we can share a list of likes, an easy conversation,
a message metronome, almost like a passage of time. You,
a silhouette known only to a meandering of fingers

across silent space, the desire of fire pressed into silk.
The distance of you hanging like a paper snowflake
unfolded delicately and placed in the window

of my mind as I yearn for a winter wonderland of you. I
just   want to fall into your eyes
and take you with   me.

How many hours until the air between us is divvied up
at our lips? A kiss to say everything we never could.
A history of distance   melts. Touch becomes

our new memory. My hands in your earth will draw spring,
a pile of tangerines at our toes, each moment
citrus sweet, our shadows made of legs and laughter.

Come hither sweet woman and climb up the world with me,
I have arms and a home for you.
Let's find freedom on the seas.
I will love you until the flowers of light within you
bloom
                  and make the sun blush.

Silence surrounds everything I've ever had of you.
A thousand days until you light my sky with your candles
electricity dancing on fingertips as we breathe.

I am not supposed to. Believe.

clouds wander between their destinations
above a devil that knows he isn't allowed to be any good,
as my fingers brush the hair from her big eyes,

a machete slicing a jungle to find and free her beast.
i wish her thoughts were cavemen and i, talented flint,
making hell impotent and wish for rain.

clouds stick to one plane for their entire lives
thinking a compass points to every movement possible.
they find their right and wrong in north and south

and their rebellion to the west. not understanding that self awareness
means you are who you were that moment that   you knew.
trapped in a circle saying who i was is who i am. i am afraid

of unraveling the line straight to what i want because
not all women are called isabella or have curves that
tame time into a cadence singing songs   for her.

stuffed inside me i have a cold sticky mind on edge
watching her pass with flesh too damned to be saved even by fingers
reaching far enough to dream desire for what   could be.

i am stuck on a plane traveling in a direction
discernible only from moment to moment.
if i am what i was i will be without a woman called isabella

and the devil will never know what it is to be any good.

J.T. Kade

Before anything else becomes of the day
I become an ocean grabbing at your shores intently,
a rhythm whispering to the nerves of your animals
too primitive to dream of ever being dry,
yet always wishing for their final baptism,
like I wish for your   love.

Every morning I dress myself in the highest sun of Siena,
the one in August pressing down on the back of galloping horses.
With that light hanging in my eye I want to set your sweat racing.
So I step into the day with a gait that is the reason
that tobacco is in cologne. A swagger of shoulders
and my bones become soldiers wrestling
in the dreams sung by long bodies ready with riddles
of skin   untangled by my momentum.

I just want to stop the winds of heaven
from visiting your face too roughly.

I wish when you passed me you had swimming pool eyes
with a neighborhood fence easily jumped by "hello beautiful."
You slip into my head intoxicating all my good senses,
your sunrise overwhelms my day with colors
leaving outlines of Roman empires in the horizons
underneath my nerves.

When we part it leaves me in your dark, aging.

My mind is a dusty museum:
white hills and breasts, educated hips,
an ancient history of lips invaded by armies of girls next door,
the clay of skin, my potters hands,
the first time I knew the taste,
the hunger it multiplied.

But you, you make me want to unravel the world into a pile of threads
to create a bed where we could live and die celebrating
the loss of our worries with drums.
I watch the curves you cut into space with hunger,
see the places on your neck I want to parachute to
so I can belay down your back with the ropes of my mouth and make camp at
your sweet   yes.

I wear my want for you like humidity.
Your weather is my season, your moon tilts my oceans,
every time I touch your mouth my dreams become the day.
As you cross and uncross your legs
you become a file that rubs against the chains
of my being a man.
You make me forgive forgiveness
because the angels of your body leave me wanting.

Please.

Lets slip into something and never recover.

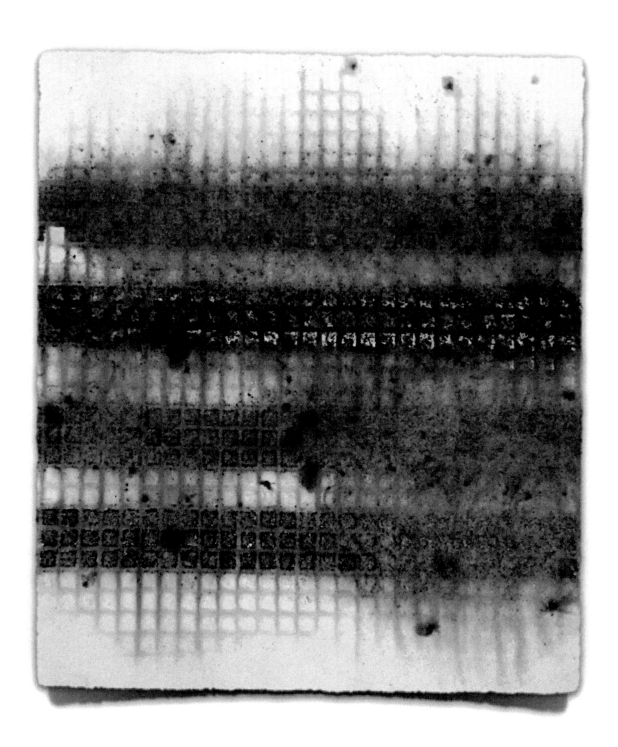

Midnight breathing on
silken calculated necks,
a perforated violent kind of adoration
worn not owned.

The pain of fresh beauty,
a woman blue in a white gown,
that I follow like eyes
lost to the wind.

I am afraid. Cold hearted I reach
for how she feels. I say
to her neck, "I've lived
my life confined by my fear of you."

Her eyes could
make a fool of us all,
but she smiles and says
"join me."

Did I become what
I deserved or what
she did? Do we ever
have any say?

When you touch one thing with deep awareness, you touch everything.

- Lao Tzu

Untitled (Love)

Love is a night where details
melt like butter blessing your fingertips with sweetness,
a soft softness, a languid dance, memory of gold,
skin as a way to God and religion.

Laughter is forgiveness, eyes an ability,
the whisper of hello is all the seduction ever needed.
A history of arms and legs inter
twined in stories that have already been written

Leave the air between a prayer echoed by the heart
that knows one thing "I just want to be good
to you. Come   closer." Easy as a second kiss easy,
easy as the warmth of fire in the cold of winter easy,

Like a yellow flower tucked behind your ear for Easter.
The moment is holy water poured slow,
time measured by checking the hour of eyes,
the breath on your neck, the simplicity of the day,

and the distance of mouths.

I want to hear you say:
do to me what spring does to cherry trees.
Let it drip syllable honey from your mouth,
create fairytales of Roman hills and lovers
who believe in believing.

I'll take a breath, explore the floor, and look back up   to you.
I'll hide the million bees buzzing beneath my cheeks
and pull at every molecule of time I can
to kiss you longer than long, and slow.

I want to jump from a great height after a hard war,
soar through the sky to find you,
a sweet balm for my leather weary.

I will hold you like you aren't the last chopper out of 'Nam;
You are 'Nam. My country.
I will stay your battles warm with home.

I want my Sunday morning filled
with the electricity of your fruit.
Long rays of sunshine,
breath mingled with the humidity of after.

I will make jazz in pans and scallions,
find your gentle in the sunrise,
and whisper until your nerves
                         ready.

I want to use one finger to brush the hair from your eyes,

to fall as rain from a blue cloud,
splash off your green only to land again,
softer and more firm each time.

I will find my humility in your roots,
forget the warmth of the sun and sweat against you,
thirst completely forgotten.

I want lips that know that shade is not meant for them,
time together weightless and full of waterslides,
the moment wet and ready for adventure.

There is a moon hidden behind our tongues,
a world of colors that kaleidoscope and ballet
in the rhythm of fat violins.

Let me call you beautiful once.

Once.

Linger on your gaze that gains my temperature,
fire tracing the oxygen met by our eyes slick
with intention.

I want you to emerge from the night,
a bashful half smile, find the inside that is   beside me,
blood running, our adventure.

But most   of all, I want to believe in the wild west of you,
undiscovered, hills of gold.

Let's damn this weather and wave our flag for freedom.

I will drive wild horses across mad landscapes towards
horizons   of you.

Pay times price,
                and work your earth for spring.

Epithalamion

Lost in the shade of the cold sun
it is your love that has found me,
a whispering song climbing fertile hills,
with eyes that I spill into, I've climbed into,
like a flower finding spring.
Our nomadic embraces build castles of memory;
I peer from the towers to wish upon stars
passing through my simple skin.
Our days are sweet and long as honey in the shade.
When you leave my organs go with you,
holding warm your heart, nature, and I come true.
Living in the gardens of moments
left floating in the air of your wake,
my stomach full,
my storming thoughts still.
I wrap around the world of colors
you painted inside a monochrome past.
Help me raise my wooden sails, and naked,
set course for the shores of dreams
woven into our everything.

With this, your fingers are my roots,
Your pulse the only time I know.
I'll keep my breath warm with love,
Your touch is now my home.

You,
      needing moments of still, held   tight,
taking in the air like holy water poured slow.

Pause.

I love you for how you look   right now.
Don't move, but move like you do. Don't say anything
besides everything you want to.

Skin is more than a gift, it's my discovery of land,
my nature dancing in the break
of a forest, letting gold sun cover my body.
No matter the winter, I believe in your summer.

Easy like that, a feather floating to ground.

We tied our hearts to the sun
   and flirted with the moon.

I love you to love you
cause I've the chance
to love you.

rain washes away what the sun can't touch,
smiles from her sparkle, summer's candles,
burning brightly on the altar of the ocean
during sunny days. her days.
maybe if i'm eight today i'll believe i will reach them
by swimming underneath the waves of anticipation.
maybe i will reach them.   maybe today.

but life doesn't work that way anymore,
now that i have hair in the wrong places,
thoughts far from "can matt come out and play?"
all those mornings i shoveled my grown-upness
on the softest parts of my brain wanting to sleep in.
some days i think god is cruel cause
he didn't bring this life to me earlier
when i had time to build tree forts to test the rain,
dreams of being a surgeon so i could see inside my workings,
why didn't i realize how nice a sunny day could be?

now   i know.
i see it in her when she looks up from her papers,
a glimpse of my nerves after my first kiss
after my first fumbling in the dark for buttons,
the first time I played her curves and she smiled,
leaving my spine a kite flying in her wind
watching her child eyes for a gust and a chance to rise.

When you plant a seed of love, it is you that blossoms.
-Ma Jaya Sati Bhagavati

Golden gossamer,
a melody of her   light.

The breeze turns in her preference
carrying stars that don't   blink,

eyes aren't enough to reflect
her blonde in the wind,

an endless stream of sunshine.
She climbs a tree with hope unfurled

-a sun hanging below the rest
taking root in a drop of dew

resting on ethereal palms-
each finger secretly a bough of apples

spiced with no new things at all,
daylight without   tricks.

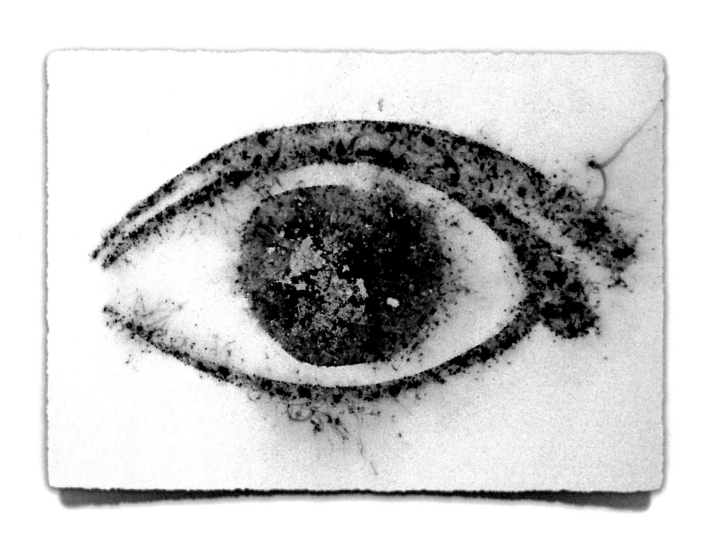

her organs resonate rooted
in the richest soil of the sun's repose:
she's laughter of a hundred headlights
rising for any reason - a fugitive sunlight -
stampeding on doors of heaven

calling to arms angels of color to dance.
she carries our shadows in her pockets
brewing potions plaited with thread,
spilling into firework fingers that weave
bolts into fortunes.

she awoke to find the ocean
in her bed asking for marriage -
the moon so close, weighted, it
forgot gravity in her gaze.

but she never forgets her magic,
she finds the shore in darkness
and whispers to the hanging moon:

Let's rise.

I wish women could pack their beauty
in a suitcase so when it tries to break
from the crowd of their skin
and multiply without cause
it is trapped in musty leather
underneath their bed.
No men to witness it,
contort into a spear,
aim at something soft,
better than themselves.

Do men just hope to be allowed
a moment of weakness,
To bend like twigs
at the sight of sexy?

Do women know
that moment as strength
or do they feel their woven
blue sweater wears them instead,
Feel thin strapped shoes
are a platform for a temple
they do not want to have as a religion,
let alone gather followers?

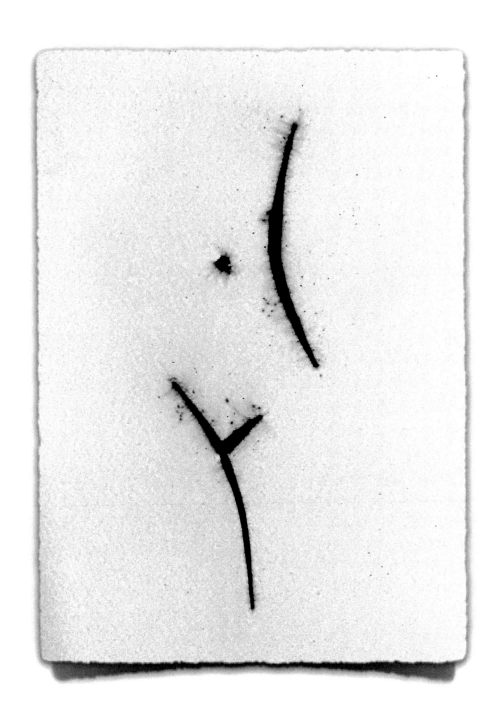

How unfair it is that stones
can handle time unnoticed,
How some women walk upon them
with their hearts in a tunnel,
Consonants in their throat.
Birds gathering around them
With mouthfuls of vowels
as her hour expands without   warning.

I feel wrong for catching her smile,
Seeing it as small yellow blade of light
Flickering at my bedside casting shadows.
I'm primitive and want to fall
from a great height   towards her,

I am a caveman hunting for wisdom
found in sticks rubbed together,
so maybe I can burn the looks
on her suitcase, wrap myself
with what's within and
multiply with   cause.

Dear You,

I want to picture you old today, in a rocking chair on our white washed porch
yelling at the kids (we used to be). I will love your grandma grumbled mutter
at the mention of fast food and your old rancid breath. You will rattle your
walker in the air every time you hear (or think you hear) loud hip hop pop
music with its gang of drums behind every beat. During the day I will find
you (seemingly or not) alone in a room talking to animals and, if you keep
going the way you have been, I know I will find you deep in a conversation
with a ficus with feelings, because I know from you it has them. I don't know
what you will eat then, how you will deal with the thought of its infant/
bulby/seedlike adorabilities forcing itself into your thoughts, like so many
thoughts do when you aren't watching. Your hair is turning white but I know
I will hear another thousand plus times about how this new young thing is a
bad example for the other things and we must not support it cause women
aren't things but stuff and you will be right and so beautiful at the same
time, every time, and I will listen. The wrinkles on your face have started
prospecting for the future, especially around those miracle nebulae eyes
I've fallen into for entire weekends. Its no wonder when I have seen the
gleam of every metal the stars are made of reflect back at me, leaving a trace
on what I am because when you smile I do, galaxies grow in our gaze. We've
wrinkled together moments of origami pastures but you don't like the East.
 You are girl with hair that rode the winds of Arizona. Remember your words
found me to your West and I climbed the lines of your poetry as if whispers
became a train denying longitude and latitude and I was a bare page looking
up at trembling fingers and a mouth that styled the world with small hopes
and dreams. I want to spend forever watching you old because my dreams pale
to the reality of every perfect you aren't and always have been. I want to do
everything on Earth with you.

Love you more tomorrow,

Me

Childhood dreams lingers longer
in the weightlessness of her smile.

I'm walking in the Sea of Tranquility, playing
hide and seek amidst the craters.

She hungers my air for intoxication
because the spin of her breeze said dance.

Every bit of the moment is her.
A forgotten kind of easy:

Live music with feet dripped in rhythm, arms alive.
Warmth teaching the ground freedom with a smile:

a kiss that begins in the center of the belly,
a neon flower trying out all the colors of nature,

Let me play amidst her shadows,
she is the moon to me.

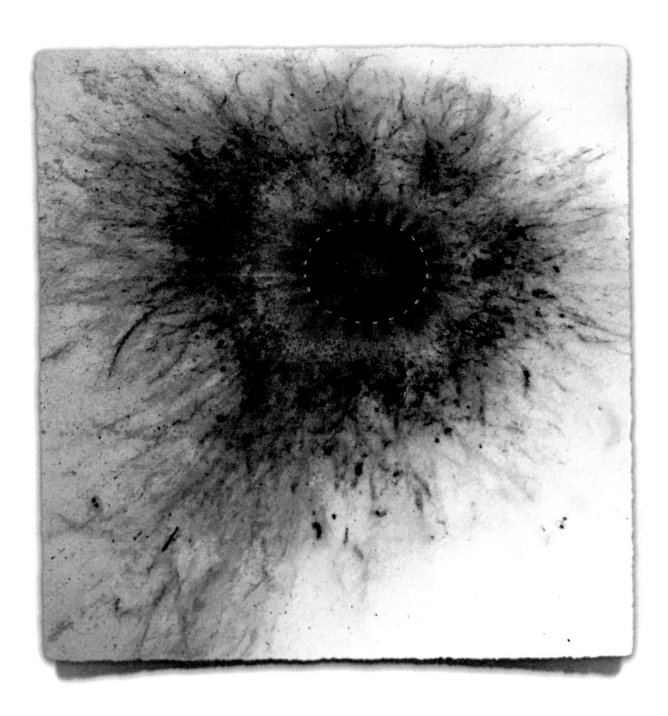

Epiphany

I was riding the last great courage
of clouds sailing the sky insulting gravity,
the day hot, hot like her with that voice.

A voice that came through passageways
breaking apart the moment with sunshine,
there she grooved with a sleepy grace in her eyes,
a kiss after dinner when you've known the meal for years.

A vision in school day recess light soaked in play
as the wild five limbed pocket spiders
invited color to dance with their instruments,
and she was their rainbow.

Buttery blonde tones hung on the air,
fireflies at midnight, but midday,
dancing like they knew the stars
in the ocean should surround us.

The gloss of her lips sighed
kiss me and you'll never do homework again.
Epiphany sweet in her eyes
my mouth wrapped spicy hungry words,
a kid in puberty with a B average and a cool best friend.

If I let my brain sweat and dance
maybe she will see me,
and we will slow cook into the evening sky.

When the heart speaks, the mind finds it indecent to object.
-Milan Kundera

Somedays I can go nearly an hour
without thinking about the taste of your mouth.
I imagine a new country,   your body,
learning the slow sounds
of the sunset where,
at this moment,
my thoughts turn to the night.

Maybe you'll be out,
With eyes deep as two moons resting in the water
painting the shore with your hips.

I remember the shape of your neck
the first time you slept next to me,
I stared until I poured all over   you,
until my blood turned to rain.

Your skin was like Saturday as I called out to you,
sleeping, with only the slow sound of my sigh
and fire of my fingers.

I miss waking to the intricate flicker of thoughts chiming in your eyes.

Some things just take root in the brain and never let go.

Missing you is like
hearing your name sung softly behind me.
I turn with hope of seeing you,
to say, tie me up with you and leave no room, please.
But desire leaves only a   dent in the air.

Woman, I miss you,
Some afternoons it's alright.
The days I know you exist and I can feel myself slipping
into moments that still linger.

But right now,
I miss you because I know you are out there   being
beautiful.

I keep your photo in my breast pocket
and speak to its' silence:
A cratered moon wrapped in gauze
that I gently press to my chest knowing

that you will not climb in my sky today.

Sometimes it catalyzes my fall to earth;
with you I was unbound,
a heart limitless,
and fingers that could see through clothes.

Your photo now, is sometimes
my weakness; and I wear my glasses all day.

Memory, pure panic.

That time I fell
trying to palm the sunrise

amidst butterfly friends
coloring the morning with dance,
spring's dew hanging
on our fingers glistening in the light.

The best days,

the ones long
with the sadness of letting go,
I feel you take my hand
and I dream of showing
our children
this young
too beautiful you
as they gather around

                              our fire.

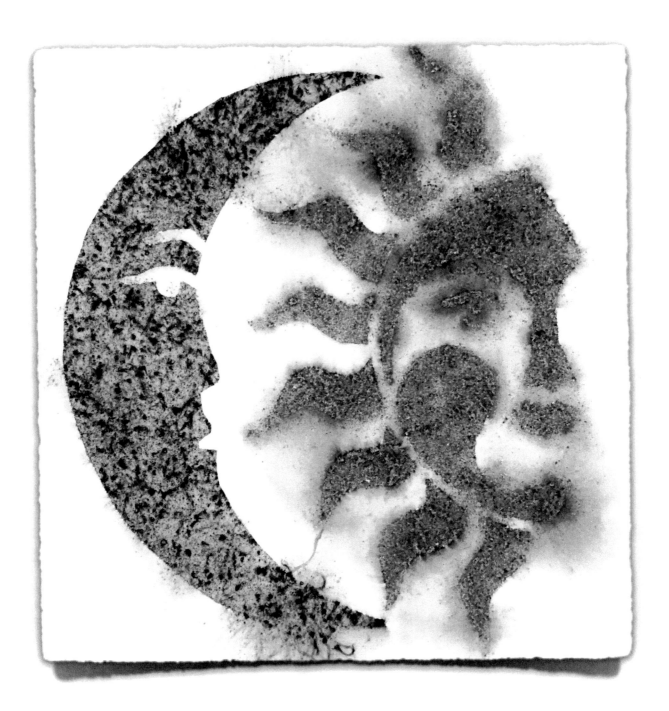

I am weighed down by what I tried and couldn't say to you.
Sometimes, to say something right I need to see my
words reflect in your eyes like a mirror,
but you aren't here anymore.

For a moment time slows down as if I were praying.
I step outside to taste the sky's fat tears
and wonder if your sky cries at all.

Please forgive the way that I love you for I always will,
and perhaps it is the worst sin, vanity, to love without return
when love seems so scarce,
but I hope it is my greatest feat
so I'll fill my heart with water in case you ever became thirsty.

The sunlight awoke heaven around our shoulders once
as we rose from the twisted sheets, out of what we once were,
turning the day from something beautiful to sacred.
Remember that night we danced in black
and the days after that caused us to pause?
I wept then for I knew soon we wouldn't see
the same sky at night.
Days were ours.

I have a million whys answered inside depths of your eyes
that tell me stories of a sun and moon chasing each other with passion
only to join each of the silent blessed spheres in the same framed sky
so night would know day and I would believe the impossible,
you loved me and wanted to come back.
Memories whisper between blessing and burden,
with silence defining the beauty I have left of you.
What is beauty but a soul that can bring me to the night,
show me stars that laugh at me,
while I ponder why I get the chance to be loved,
even for a moment.

A voice within still affected by blue-eyed water
and faith in spheres you gave to me,
fade to a meaningless dream.

-Let all those who drown take my breath for it has lost all purpose-

I can still taste your mouth and play music to the rhythm of sun
as it climbed up your body at sunrise.
But I don't listen to your songs anymore,
I just miss you.

Woman when it comes to love I choose passion and pain.
I know I've lost you
I dream someday I'll find you again.

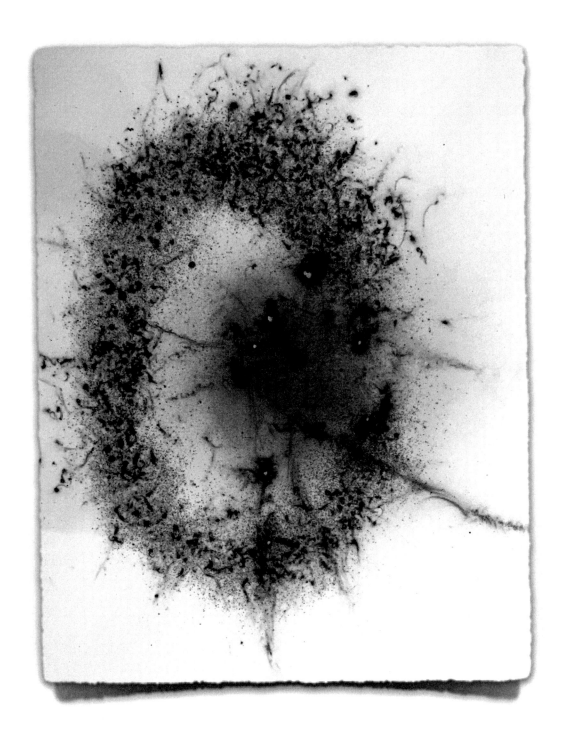

It's them,
that leave us,
that never come back,
cause we don't fight.

In honor unsheathe our mettle and say
                "Without love it is only life..."

The purest act
is with short swords,
splitting open our revelation,
to leave our organs where we slump
along with the idea of the thing,
not to be found hiding
between the shadow
and the act.
No mercy.

Eros infused agápe recedes.

The city is cold.

The Word

you lost our child on the way back from the moon
crescent and sharp hooked in the lumpy night of befores
that turned into cold outlines of memories whispering to dwindling echoes
always leaning reluctantly/intently towards the day of afters
trapped behind open doors
that I must turn the corner

       from you

to

Love, too, was just a question of time.
-Paulo Coelho

I am sick of words. Let's skip hello.
Sick of conversations about angles,
fractions, job descriptions like plastic
foreplay. Sick of pictures of people
pretending to be people in pictures
with sly words and flickers.
I want your jungle, the dainty
monsters, the bottom of your
dark, I want them to find my caves
formed of clay and birth animals
that don't give up because I wasn't
funny one night. I want my robot
vacuum to get stuck on things
you leave behind. I am sick of
knowing that all I want to say is
I don't know how to get closer to
you, how to row that distance
between your nose just finding
mine and mine just finding yours
and this ocean that just sits here
between fingers, phones, tables,
clothes, everything that feels clean.
Touch sometimes feels like a
typewriter and I try real hard
to pay attention to my grammar but
can we not do that?

Replace moans with your roar and move
like we get to party with the privilege
of a hangover - both sides of gravity
giving us their blessing but making
it dirty so we don't forget to.
What's all this language? Can't we just
remember that the tongue is far superior
to the words it shapes? That just one
night with each other
can create cities filled
with skyscrapers of yes
and traffic jams of when
can I see you again?

So in lieu of hello,
when can I see you again
for the first time?

About the Work:

When I was 11 years old my English teacher asked everyone to read a poem in class. I was the shortest, smallest kid with a haircut my mom was proud of and knit sweaters with graphic depictions of golf and horses hiding the well tucked polo shirt underneath. I was called cute. I hated it.

My older brother had forgotten a book of poetry he was reading and I managed to stumble upon it. It was creased open to a page with a line that said "if sex is electric this couple was wired." I was beside myself with the find. That was the poem I read in class...at least the first 5 stanzas of it before my teacher stopped me. Something about that reading changed me. I learned the power of words and I gained the acceptance of everyone around me because I read it like I knew it was the coolest thing I'd ever say.

One of the characters in the poem was J.T. Kade. He loved a woman and went crazy because he attempted to tame her rather than dive into love full force. My book is in part inspired by his lessons, the poetry of Tim Seibles and Pablo Neruda, and all of my experiences of love and loss.

I have spent years writing the words and refining them with the help of some of the best people I could ask for. This is my attempt to celebrate love using both poetry and art created with the use of gunpowder. I chose such an unruly form because love is unpredictable and never tamed. I think we all need more beauty in our days, and perhaps better ways to speak about it, this is simply my small addition.

For art and inquiries:

www.jtkade.com/art

For audio of the poems:

www.jtkade.com/trueloveandsmoke

Password: samcooke

Dedications

I Am Not Supposed To Believe - Dobramira, Karimé
First Love - Sarah
Untitled (Love) - Mika
I Want - Lauren
Epithalamion - Krista & Pat Sheehan
Lost Youth - Dorothy
No New Things - Sam
M.S. - Mallory
To Be - Karen
Smile - Megan
Epiphany - Amy and The Engine
Woman, I Miss You - Jeein
Photo - Leslie
Woman, If I Had Words - Mia

Acknowledgements:

Thank you to Zach Morriss, Gerd Schmidt, Phillip Hurzeler, Jack Spencer, Patrick Sheehan, Thom Lager, Colin Ryan, Martha Erwin, Benjamin Creisher, Kristopher Tillery, Karen Song, Glenn Hudson, Mikki Columbus, Lewis Ford, Jacob Auger, Justin Delany, Isaac Pearlman, Amanda Moy, Gail Dubian, Mary Ann Adrian, Pauline Sheehan, Pepin Gelardi, Stephanie Hoos, Alec Lager, Damiano Femfert, David Ferrarini, Rudolph Skowronski, Megan Lofthus, Aaron Warren, Taylor Brady, Savannah, Van Marines, Garret McDonough, Erin Donovan and the many beautiful women and men in my life that have inspired this vision, supported it, and put up with my curious passions for the years. My heart is forever yours. And of course, thank you Mom.

"To describe my mother would be to write about a hurricane in its perfect power. Or the climbing, falling colors of a rainbow."
Maya Angelou

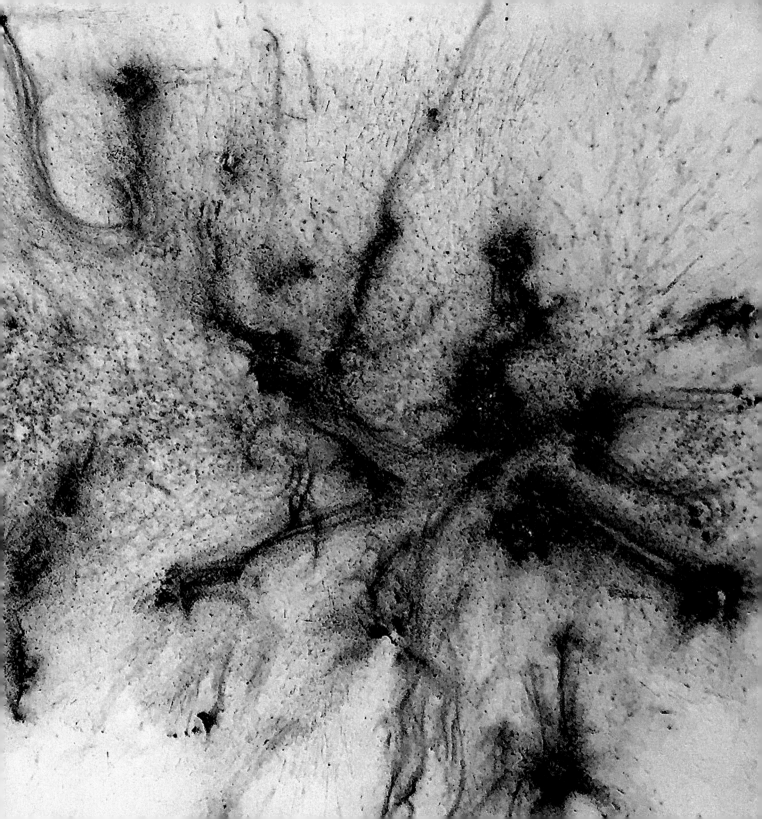

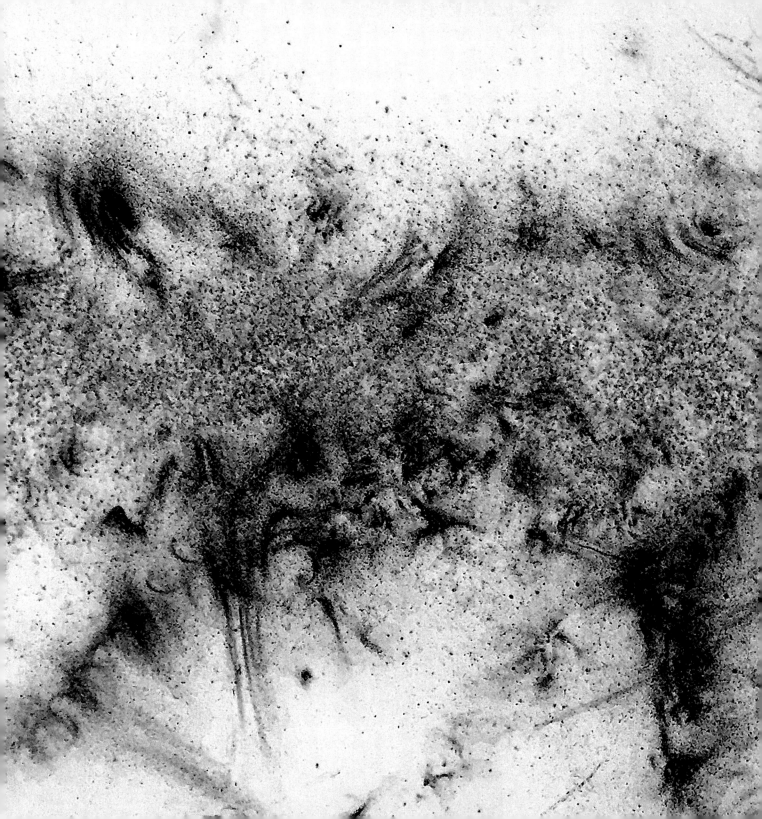

Made in the USA
Middletown, DE
08 April 2016